KENYA

Welcome to Kenya.

I hope you enjoy learning all about my home country of Kenya and that you find it as fascinating a country as I do. This book is packed with facts and information about Kenya. Whilst using this book, you will also learn many geographic skills along the way.
Enjoy!

Published in 2014, 2021

Copyright © Ian Jeffery
Written and designed by Ian Jeffery
Illustrations by Shutterstock

Printed in the United Kingdom by KDP.

Contents

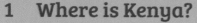

Where is Kenya?

To find out where places are, we use a **map**. A book with lots of maps in is called an **atlas**. There are many different types of maps. Some maps show the weather. Some maps display roads, railways and towns. Whereas others show rivers, lakes and mountains.

This is a **physical map**. It shows natural features like rivers, lakes, deserts and mountains.

This is a **political map**. It shows man-made features like towns, countries and borders.

What **features** can you think of which will be shown on physcial maps and human maps?

Your tasks:

You are going to use an atlas to find out more about where Kenya is.

1 In your atlas, find a human map of Kenya .
2 Find the capital city of Kenya.
3 Count how many countries share a border with Kenya.
4 What is the name of the ocean next to Kenya?

Kenya is in East Africa.

1

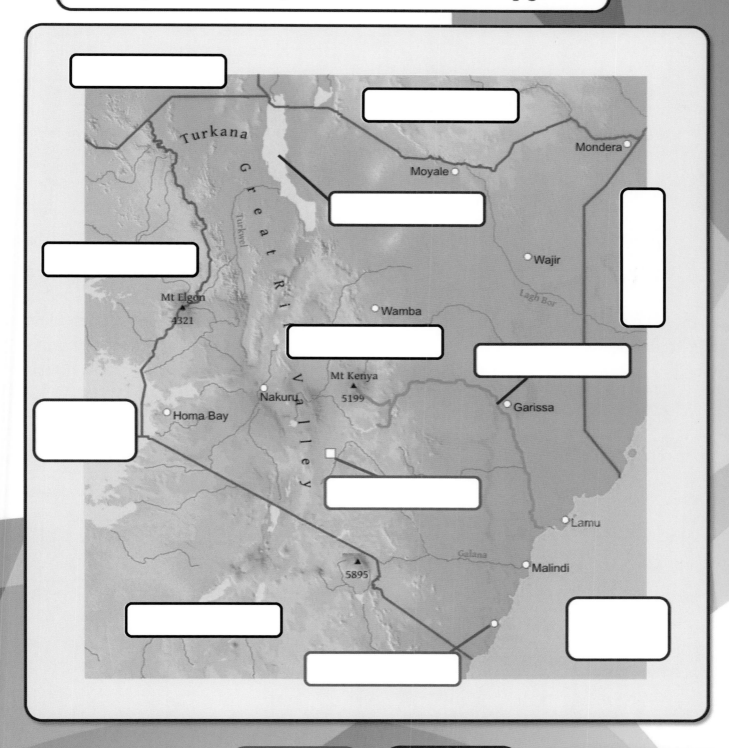

Geography skill covered in this activity:

Using an atlas

Cities
Nairobi
Mombasa

Water features
Lake Turkana
Lake Victoria
Indian Ocean
Tana River

Countries
Tanzania   Ethiopia
Kenya   Uganda
Somalia
South Sudan

Getting to Kenya

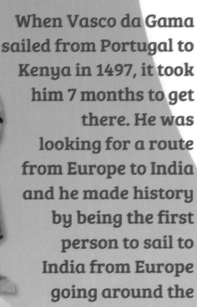

When Vasco da Gama sailed from Portugal to Kenya in 1497, it took him 7 months to get there. He was looking for a route from Europe to India and he made history by being the first person to sail to India from Europe going around the Cape of Good Hope. When he arrived in Kenya he was met with hostility and he soon carried on his way.

By the 1860s, the fastest sailing ships ever built, the great tea clippers could sail from England to Kenya in 66 days and when the Suez canal opened in 1869, this cut the journey to 47 days. An average ship going throught the Suez canal in

2013 pays £150,000 to travel the 193 kilometres through the canal, however, shipping companies save money by having shorter routes and spending less time at sea so they always chose the Suez route.

With the advance of modern technology, a modern container ship can make the same journey from Kenya to England in 8 days and 19 hours.

But why sail when you could take a plane? Queen Elizabeth II was on holiday in Kenya when she found out that her father had passed away and she had become Queen. Her flight home in 1952 took over 19 hours. The same journey today can be done in 11 hours and 15 minutes.

? Technology is improving all the time. What do you think the journey will be like in 100 years time?

Measuring distances on maps

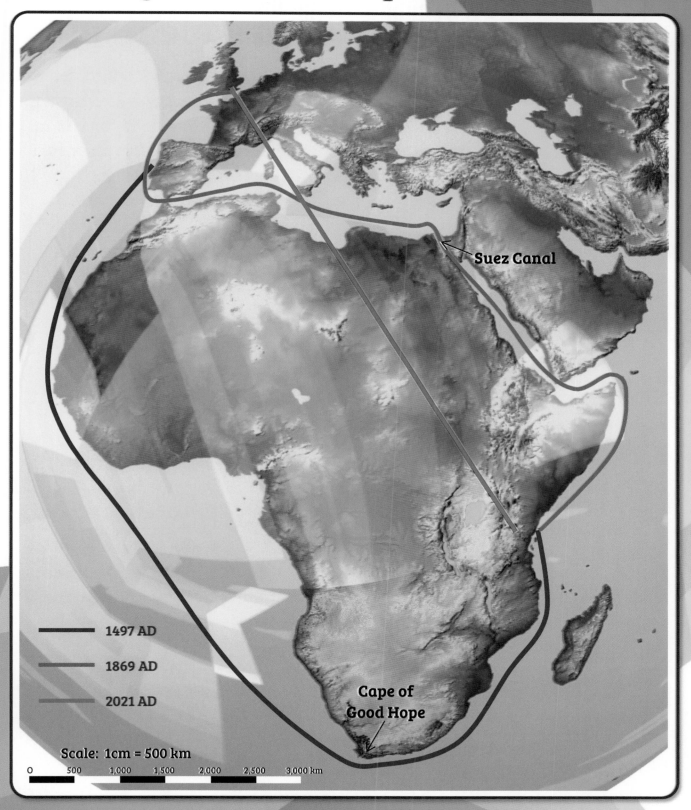

1497 AD

1869 AD

2021 AD

Suez Canal

Cape of
Good Hope

Scale: 1cm = 500 km

0   500   1,000   1,500   2,000   2,500   3,000 km

Geography skill
covered in this activity:

Measuring
curved-line
distances

Your Task:
Using a piece of string and the scale line, measure the
distances marked on this map by the different routes.

What is the landscape like?

Kenya is a large country with a wide variety of different landscapes. From the wide, grassy savannahs to the mountainous forests, from the beautiful beaches to the rift valley, there are many beautiful places to visit and see.

Kenya's beaches are beautiful and draw many tourists every year.

Kenya has temperate hills in the west which are fertile and great for growing crops like tea as shown in this picture.

Kenya has tall mountains with snow on all year round.

A savannah is a grass land environment with the rain falling mostly in one season. The trees do not make a continuous canopy.

Drawing a field sketch is an important skill. You need to identify the main features from a landscape and draw them in a simpler, easy to understand way. Then you label your diagram as shown in this example below. Remember to always give your work a title.

The Savannah in Kenya

Trees are spaced apart.

Rolling hills that are not forested.

Large areas of flat land

Trees grow tall to avoid giraffes.

Arid land due to low rainfall

Thorny bushes prevent being eaten

Geography skill covered in this activity:

Making a field sketch

Your Task:
Make a field sketch of the landscape shown in the picture above. Give your field sketch labels and a title.

Learning objective:
We are going to learn where Kenya is. We are also going to learn what maps are and how to use one.

Your Task:
Read these sentences about Kenya. Sort them into three paragraphs that are focused on one of the following topics:
(a) Geographical features of Kenya,
(b) The wildlife of Kenya,
(c) The Maasai Mara people.
The first two have been done for you.

The Kenyan highlands are one of the most successful farming regions in Africa. **a**

The "Big Five" animals of Africa can be found in Kenya: the lion, leopard, buffalo, rhinoceros and elephant. ◯

The Maasai people live a traditional life and the end of life is virtually without ceremony, with the dead left out for scavengers to eat. **c**

Black rhinos used to be numerous in Kenya until poaching reduced their numbers. There are only 5,400 left. ◯

It is so tall that it has glaciers on its top, even in summer. ◯

The measure of someone's wealth is in terms of cattle and children. ◯

The men in the Maasai tribe are born and raised to be warriors. ◯

In 2019, the Maasai population reached 1,189,522 people. ◯

It is hot all year round and summer clothes are worn throughout the year. ◯

When Writing in paragraphs, we don't indent the first one.

7

Hippopotami and Nile crocodiles can be found in large groups in the Mara and Talek rivers.

Kenya's climate varies from hot and wet (tropical) along the coast to hot and dry (arid) in the north.

Maasai society is strongly patriarchal with the elder men, deciding most major matters for each Maasai group.

Over 11 million animals migrate a distance of 2,800 km searching for food and water.

Mount Kenya is the highest mountain in Kenya at 5,199 m tall.

Kenya is the setting for one of the Natural Wonders of the World – the great wildebeest migration.

Your task:

Now you have sorted them according to their topic, place them into an order that makes sense when you read them aloud.

Lastly, write these three paragraphs into your exercise book.

Once you have finished your writing, you can make your work even better by adding labelled pictures and facts.

The giraffe is the tallest animal in the world.

English skill covered in this activity:

Writing in paragraphs

Weather is the condition of the air around us. It includes characteristics like temperature, rainfall, wind speed and cloud cover.

What are the different ways we can find out the weather?

You could listen to a weather forecast on the **radio**.

You can read a weather forecast in a **newspaper**.

You could look **online**.

You could use an **app** on your phone.

In the days before all our modern technology, people would look out the **window** and decide what the weather was going to be like. Can you think of some of the difficulties that this might cause?

You could watch a weather forecast on the **television**.

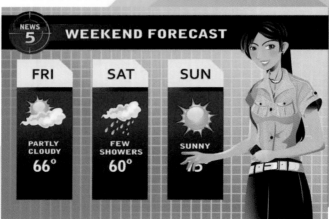

? What is the weather like where you are today?
And what is the weather like in Kenya today?

Your Task:
Find out what the weather will be like in Kenya and where you are today.
Compare your findings. Use the table below to record your results.

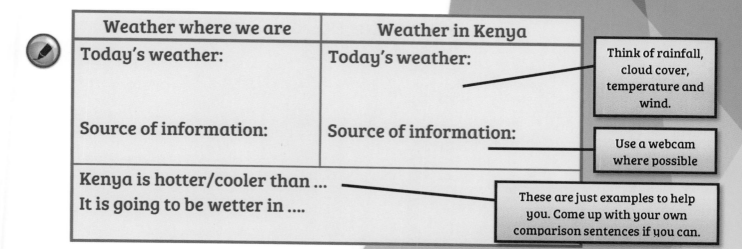

Weather where we are	Weather in Kenya
Today's weather:	Today's weather:
Source of information:	Source of information:
Kenya is hotter/cooler than ... It is going to be wetter in	

Think of rainfall, cloud cover, temperature and wind.

Use a webcam where possible

These are just examples to help you. Come up with your own comparison sentences if you can.

? Now we need to look at our weather words. How many words can you think of to describe rainfall? Can you think of different ways to describe a cloudy day?

Your Task:
Using a thesaurus to help you and working in pairs, build up a list of words that you can use to describe the weather. How many words can you find?
Place your words into similar groups. See below for examples.

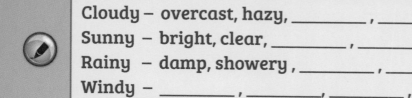

Cloudy – overcast, hazy, _____ , _____
Sunny – bright, clear, _____ , _____
Rainy – damp, showery , _____ , _____
Windy – _____ , _____, _____ ,

You could look up these words in the thesaurus to help you:
stormy, hot, cold, as well as:
sunny, cloudy, rainy, windy,

Geography skill covered in this activity:

Using secondary sources of information

? How did you do? Did you find lots of weather words?

Learning objective:

We are going to learn what climate is and how to read a climate graph.

What is the climate like in Kenya?

Climate is the average weather taken over a period of time. Here we can see the climate of Nairobi and compare it with the climate in London.

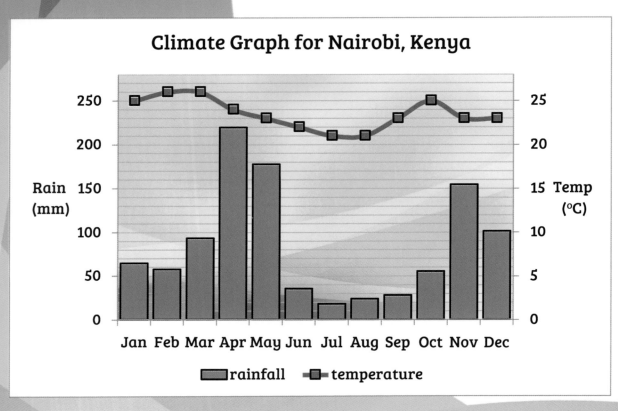

Climate Graph for Nairobi, Kenya

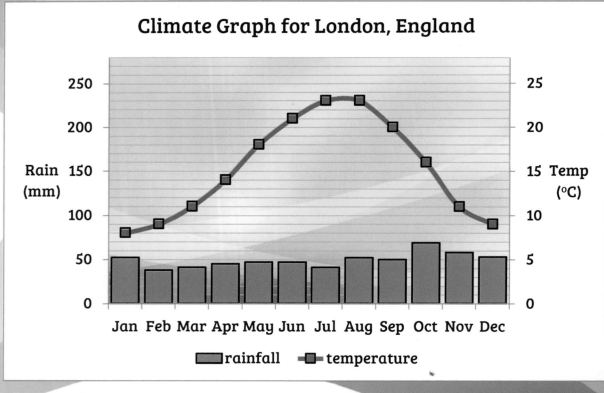

Climate Graph for London, England

Check it out

What are the hottest two months in Nairobi? _____ and _____

What are the coldest two months in Nairobi? _____ and _____

What are the hottest two months in London? _____ and _____

What are the coldest two months in London? _____ and _____

What are the two wettest months in Nairobi? _____ and _____

What are the two wettest months in London? and

Practice

How much rain falls in January in London? _____

How much rain falls in October in London? _____

How much rain falls in December in Nairobi? _____

What is the temperature in London in July? _____

What is the temperature in Nairobi in July? _____

What is the temperature in Nairobi in December? _____

> Remember: You must write 'mm' after your answer.

> Have you written '⁰C' as part of your answer?

Challenger

> Write in full sentences in this section.

Describe the rainfall pattern in London.

_____

Describe the rainfall pattern in Nairobi.

_____

Describe how the temperatures in London compare with those in Nairobi.

_____

_____

Explain how the rainfall in Nairobi will affect the plantlife in Nairobi.

_____

_____

Geography skill covered in this activity:

Reading climate graphs

Your Tasks:
Read the questions above.
Write the answers in your exercise book.

Remember that you read the rainfall on one side and the temperature on the other.

Learning objective:

In this lesson, you are going to identify which animals live in Kenya and what they look like.

Kenyan animals

Do penguins live in Kenya? Or ostriches? How do you know? How can we find out what animals live in Kenya? And what does a wildebeest look like? To answer these questions and more, we are going to look into which animals live in Kenya and then produce interesting pictures of them using online photo editors.

In your computer's web browser, open these two websites:

https://www.3dgeography.co.uk/kenyan-animals

> Tells you which animals live in Kenya.

www.befunky.com

> An online photo editor

Your tasks:

1. First upload the photo you want to work with.
   Your teacher will tell you where the photos are located.

2. Second, use the featured effects to edit your photo.
   Browse through the different effects to choose one you like.

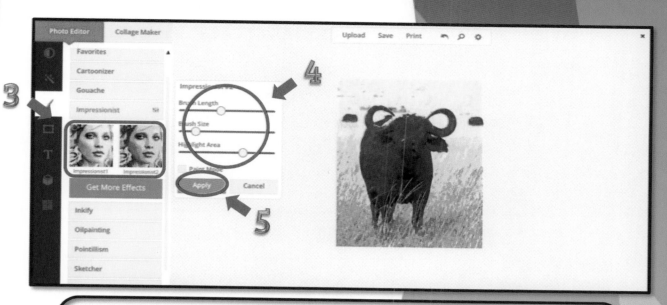

3. Browse through the different options available and select.

4. Use the sliders to edit your picture to your choosing.

5. Once you have chosen your selection, press 'apply'.

6. Add a border to your picture.

7. Write the name of your animal on your picture.

8. Save and print your work. You are finished. Good job.

IT skill covered in this activity:

Using image manipulation software

Well done. You have learnt a new skill today. Why don't you try to do this with one of your family photos at home? But do remember to ask an adult for help first so you do not accidentally delete some family photos.

Kenyan wildlife
Grid references

Kenya is famous for its wildlife and there is a wide range of animals living in Kenya that you can see when you go on safari.

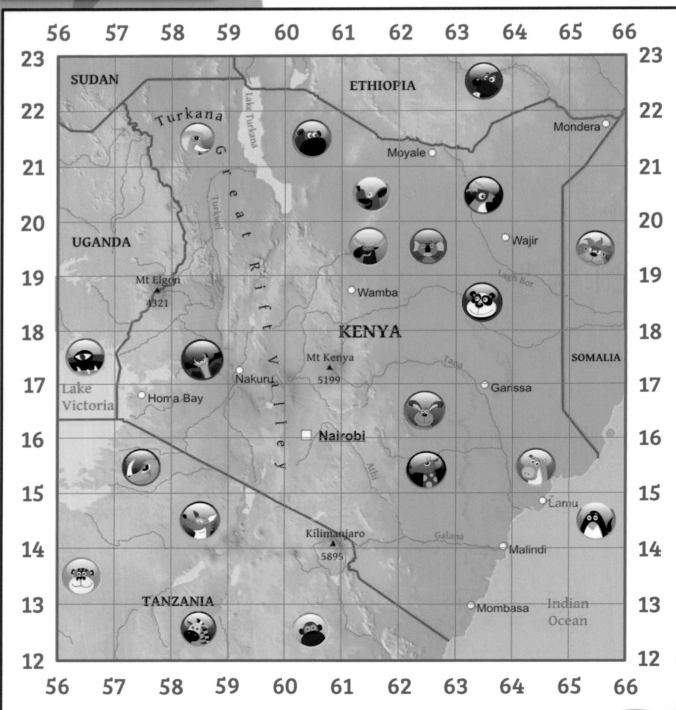

We use grid squares to locate features on a map. Can you locate where the animals are on this map? Can you say which grid square the animals are in?

These are called four figure grid references.

15

Name of animal	Grid reference	Found in Kenya		Name of animal	Grid reference	Found in Kenya
beaver		Yes/no		koala		Yes/no
gazelle		Yes/no		jackal		Yes/no
elephant		Yes/no		elk		Yes/no
bear		Yes/no		bat		Yes/no
crocodile		Yes/no		panda		Yes/no
hyena		Yes/no		rabbit		Yes/no
rhino		Yes/no		giraffe		Yes/no
tiger		Yes/no		hippo		Yes/no
zebra		Yes/no		monkey		Yes/no
lion		Yes/no		penguin		Yes/no

 How can we find out whether an animal lives in Kenya?
What are the different ways we can find out?

Your task:
1 Complete the table above by writing in the four figure grid references for each animal.
2 Draw a circle around yes or no depending on whether you can find that animal in Kenya.

 Geography skill covered in this activity:

 Using four figure grid references.

Kenyan wildlife

In this activity, we are going to make animal facts posters. You will find out some information about one animal in Kenya and present that information in an interesting way.

Here is some information you might like to find out and include in your animal facts posters:

- The size of your animal.
- The speed of your animal.
- What your animal eats.
- How they hunt their prey.
- Any special features your animal has.
- The habitat in which your chosen animal lives.

 What interesting ways can you think of presenting your animal? You could try making a finger puppet.

Task One Research	**Which animals live in Kenya?** For your first task, you need to find out which animals live in Kenya and then choose one animal that interests you. You can use the internet and library books or encyclopaedias to find out which animals live in Kenya.
Task Two Research	**Find ten facts on your chosen animal.** Once you have done some reading about your chosen animal, you need to record 10 interesting facts about your animal. Try to vary your facts. For example, try to include information on: where it lives; what it eats and key features of their appearance.

Task Three
Artwork

Draw, paint or make your animal.

Draw or make your chosen animal. Be creative. Think of different ways you can present your animal. Perhaps use different colours to the ones that you would expect to see it in or draw your animal in an interesting pose.

Task Four
Present your facts

Make your animal facts poster.

Using a piece of A3 size paper or card, place your animal in the middle of poster. Give your poster a title and write your name on your poster. Write the facts around your animal picture. Think of an imaginative way of laying out your poster.

Important information to include in your poster.

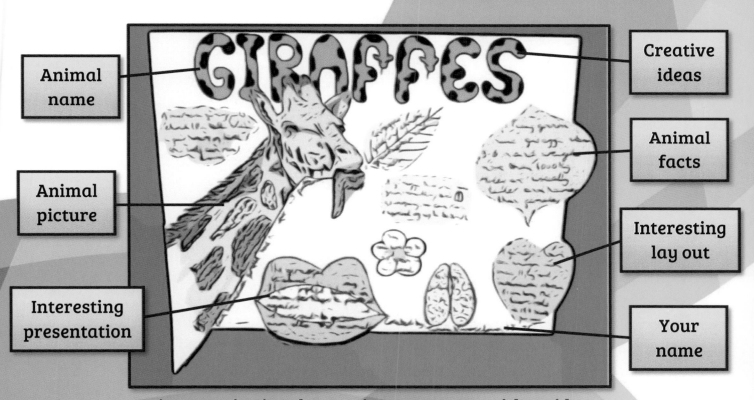

Being creative involves trying to come up with an idea that is different. You can get ideas from all around you.

Geography skill covered in this activity:
Using secondary sources of information.

? In this activity, you used reference books and the internet to find out information. Were you successful? And how good was your presentation?

Learning objective:

In this lesson, we are going to learn about what some Kenyan homes are like and how they are made.

What are Kenyan settlements like?

Can you spot ten differences between this house and yours?

The earliest Maasai were **nomads** which meant that they moved from place to place in the search of good feeding ground for their cattle. This meant that **Maasai** homes are not designed to be permanent.

When building their homes, the Maasai use materials that can find locally and this helps to make their houses environmentally friendly.

The framework of the house is formed of large, long timber poles that are hammered into the ground. Following this, smaller wooden poles are woven into the large poles to make the walls. On the outside of these branches, a mixture of mud, sticks, grass, cow dung and ash are mixed together to make a waterproof wall covering.

The cow dung has special properties which make the walls waterproof. The house is small, measuring about 3m wide by 5m long. It is about 1.5 metres high.

Inside the house, there is a large space where the family cooks, eats, sleeps, socializes and stores food and fuel. A village of homes would be surrounded by a thick hedge of thorns. At night, the animals are brought inside the thorn hedge to protect them from wild animals.

 Can you think of which wild animals might be attacking and eating the farm animals?

There are no windows and the smoke from the fire in the house helps to keep the mosquitoes at bay. The natural materials help to make this house cool in summer and warm in winter.

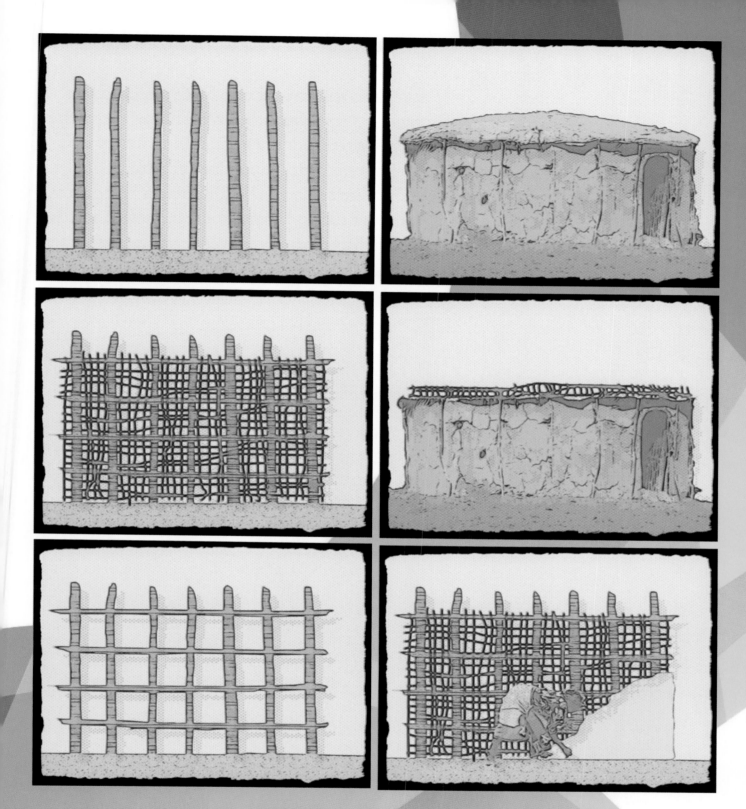

Your task:
1. Look at the images above of a Maasai home being built.
2. Place these pictures in the correct sequence for building a Maasai home.
3. Then write a description underneath each picture describing the steps involved.

Geography skill covered in this activity:

Sequencing events into chronological order.

Nairobi is the largest city in Kenya and it is home to 3.4 million people. It started when the railways came in 1899 and it is an important city in Africa with many large companies having their African headquarters in Nairobi. There are many, large, modern skyscrapers in the downtown area and there are many large modern shopping malls for people to shop in.

We call areas that are built up like Kenya **urban**. The word urban means 'related to cities'. Nairobi has many important features like an airport and a university.

The opposite of urban is called **rural**. People do live in rural areas but the settlements are small and more spread out. You will find farms and forests in rural areas.

21

? Urban areas have lots of tall buildings and lots of people. Rural areas can have lots of fields and small settlements. What other ways can you think of to describe the differences between rural and urban areas?

Your task:

1 Using a dictionary to help you, define the words rural and urban.
2 Then compare the statements below thinking of both rural and urban areas. Complete the diagram by drawing triangles to illustrate which has more. The first two have been done for you.

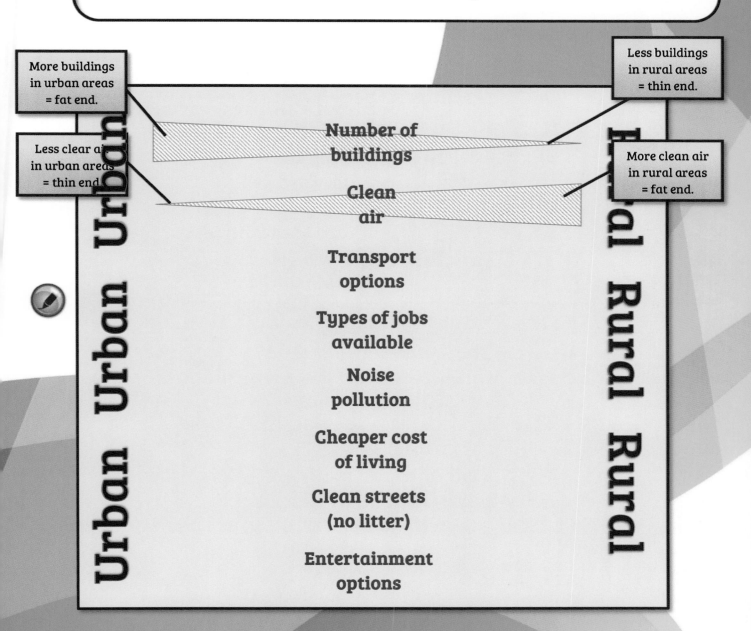

More buildings in urban areas = fat end.

Less buildings in rural areas = thin end.

Less clear air in urban areas = thin end.

More clean air in rural areas = fat end.

Urban Urban Urban

Rural Rural Rural

Number of buildings

Clean air

Transport options

Types of jobs available

Noise pollution

Cheaper cost of living

Clean streets (no litter)

Entertainment options

Geography skill covered in this activity:

Comparing one area with another: rural and urban

 Can you think of some other ways in which we can compare life in a rural area with life in an urban area?

Learning objective:

In this lesson, you are going to find out about the lives and culture of the Maasai people.

The Maasai

The Maasai are a semi-nomadic tribe of people living in Kenya and Tanzania. A traditional greeting to a member of the Maasai tribe would be "Hello. How are your cows? I hope your cows are well". This is because the Maasai's view of wealth depends on how many cows you have and the more cows you have, the wealthier you are.

Warriors - The maasai warriors believe that the higher a man can jump, the stronger he is and we can see a Maasai warrior impressing his friends with his energetic jumping. The Maasai warriors had a fearsome reputation for fighting and whilst they are well known for their spears and shields, it is their club, the orinka, that can be thrown lethally over a distance of 100m.

A man proves his strength.

A Maasai warrior.

Old age - Most matters in the Maasai community are decided by the elder men of the tribe. If a fine or penalty has to be paid, it will be paid in cattle. When someone dies, their body is left out in the open for scavengers to feed on. If the dead body is not eaten by scavenging animals, it brings embarrassment onto the family so it would not be uncommon to smear the dead body with blood from a cow.

Wealth - Traditional Maasai values centre around the owning of cattle as cows are the main source of food for the Maasai. A herd of 50 cattle is a respectable number and the more children, the better. A person with lots of cows and no children is considered poor. As the animals are looked after by the children, a man with no children has no one to look after his cattle.

A village elder.

Maasai Jewellery - Both men and women wear bracelets and bead jewellery. The bead work, made by the women, has a long history in the Maasai culture. The colours have meanings, for example, white represents peace and blue represents water. The beads were originally made from local raw materials like shells, ivory, seeds, horn and metal. Now more modern glass beads are popular and the Maasai have found ways to incorporate modern technology whilst still protecting their culture.

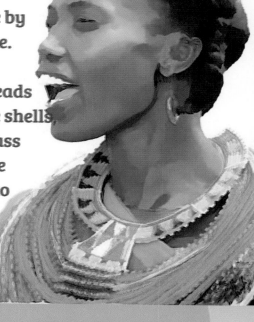

Maasai clothes - Traditionally,the Maasai would have worn clothes made from calf hides and sheep skin although clothing made from cotton is now more popular. Red is a favourite colour, with blue, black, striped and checkered patterns also being worn. Shuka is the Maasai word for sheets traditionally worn, one over each shoulder and then a third over the top of them. Maasai wear simple sandals on their feet which would have been made from cow hides but are now soled with strips of old car tyres. The Maasai have proved to be very resourceful in using those materials that they find around them. This way of life is good for the environment as it reduces waste and reuses old things.

Geography skill covered in this activity:

Drawing an annotated diagram.

Your task:
Draw an annotated diagram of a Maasai person in traditional Maasai clothing. Label your diagram to include information about the Maasai. See if you can add six or more labels to your diagram.

Learning objective:

Today we are going to learn about a day in the life of a child who lives in Kenya.

A day in the life

We are going to meet a girl called Evangeline. She lives on a shamba or a farm in in the countryside with her family. She lives close to Mount Kenya and her house is surrounded by many fields where crops such as maize, potatoes and onions are grown.

Early morning
Evangeline wakes up just after 6 o'clock in the morning and she washes herself and she gets dressed.

She feeds the calf whilst her mother makes breakfast.

Then she sits down with her mother and father to breakfast. Her older sisters are not there as they are in boarding school.

Morning
She walks to school at 7:30 am. She sometimes meets her friends along the way.

During the morning, she has lessons in school. She learns English, Maths and Geography.

Afternoon
She eats her lunch at school with her friends. She plays in the playground and after lunch, she continues to have lessons in the afternoon. Evangeline studies Art and Science and she plays sports.

After school
When she returns home from school, Evangeline helps out on the farm. She fetches water and helps out with the threshing. In the evening, the family would have dinner and relax at home, creating their own entertainment. She would be in bed by 8:00 pm.

A primary classroom in Kenya.

? In what ways is Evangeline's day similar to yours and in what ways is it different?

What time do you wake up? Have dinner? Go to bed? When do you do your homework? And do you have any sports clubs after school?

	A typical day in the life of a child in Kenya	A typical day in the life of me	
			2:00 am
			4:00 am
			6:00 am
			8:00 am
			10:00 am
			12:00 noon
			2:00 pm
			4:00 pm
			6:00 pm
			8:00 pm
			10:00 pm
			12:00 pm

Every day is different so try to pick a typical day.

Do you make your lunch? And where do you eat it?

When do you do your homework?

When do you eat dinner?

What time would you normally go to bed?

Your tasks:

Copy the table above into your exercise book.

Fill in the sections about a typical day in your life. Think about what you would do on an average day, maybe not every day. Then, complete the section for a child in Kenya. Look at what is similar and what is different.

Geography skill covered in this activity:

Recording information in a table. Making comparisons.

26

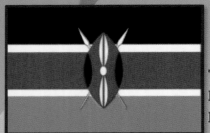

The Flag of Kenya

The national flag of Kenya

The flag of Kenya was first adopted in 1963. The colour black symbolizes the majority population, the colour red symbolizes the bloodshed during the fight for freedom and the green represents the land. The white borders symbolize peace and honesty. The black, red, and white traditional Maasai shield and the two spears symbolize the defence of the land and people.

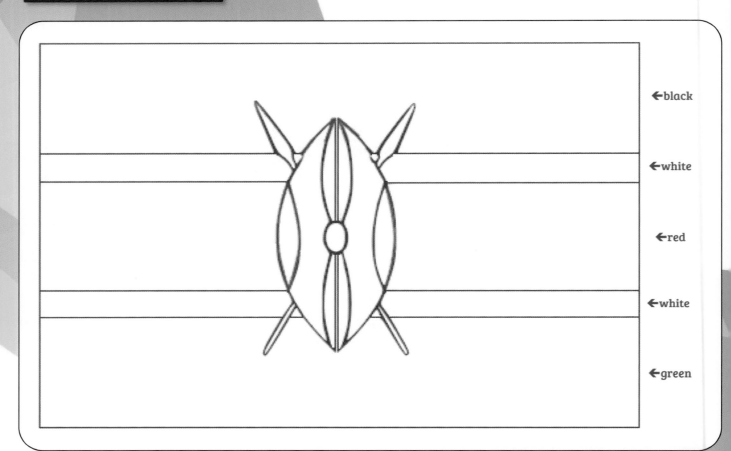

←black

←white

←red

←white

←green

Very similar to and not to be confused with these flags:

Malawi

South Sudan

Kenyan language

As many as 69 languages are spoken in Kenya but the two official languages spoken in Kenya are Swahili and English. Swahili is widely spoken throughout Africa and it is an official language in Tanzania, Uganda and the Democratic Republic of the Congo as well as Kenya.

Your tasks:
Have a look at these basic Swahili phrases and make a conversation with a friend.

Hello	Hujambo		Village	Kijiji
How are you?	Habari gani?		House	Nyumba
I am well	Mimi ni vizuri		Farm	Kilimo
Good	Nzuri		Field	Shamba
Please	Tafadhali		Food	Chakula
Thank you	Asante		Water	Maji
Yes	Ndiyo		Bread	Mkate
No	Hakuna		Banana	Ndizi
Goodbye	Kwaheri		Toilet	Choo

What is your name?	Ni nini jina yako?
My name is ...	Jina langu ni ...
Where are you going?	Unakwenda wapi?
Where do you come from?	Wapi wanatoka?
Please can you help me?	Tafadhali unaweza kunisaidia?
Can you tell me the wifi password?	Unaweza kuniambia password wifi?

I want	I unataka ..	I can't understand	Siwezi kuelewa
How much is..	Ni kiasi gani ...	Where is ....?	Ambapo ni?
Post office	Baada ya ofisi	Giraffe	Twiga
Internet café	Internet cafe	Hippopotamus	Kiboko
Police station	Kituo cha polisi	Lion	Simba

Geography skill covered in this activity: To respect the differences between our cultures and others.

How long can you make your conversation with your friend?

Decision making exercise

Tea grows well in Kenya because it has many of the conditions needed to grow good tea. The ideal conditions needed are:

- Deep, fertile, slightly acidic soil
- Rainfall spread throughout the year
- Between 1200-1400 mm of rain a year
- Long sunny days
- High altitude land

High altitude land

Tea can in fact grow at any altitude from 0m – 2,100 m. However, high land is usually cheaper as it has less alternative uses and tea plantations require a lot of land. Tea can also be farmed successfully on steep slopes. Therefore, traditionally, tea plantations have been grown in hilly areas.

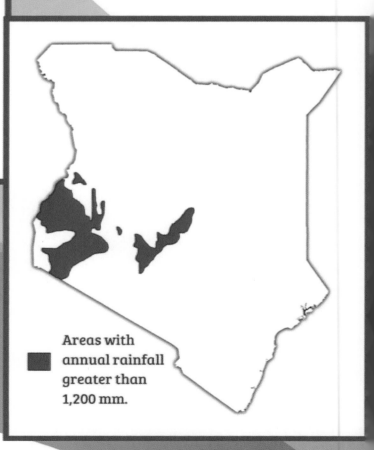

National Park

Nature Reserve

Lake

Your task:

Imagine you work for a large multinational drinks company and you have been tasked with finding the best location for a new tea plantation which your company will start. Which location do you think is best?

Areas with annual rainfall greater than 1,200 mm.

Your tools:

- You have four maps here that your company have given you to help you.
- Your class teacher will also give you some tracing paper.
- You can use coloured pencils or felt tip pens and an eraser.

Your task:

Working in twos or threes, select the best location for your new tea plantation. Explain your reasons for your location.

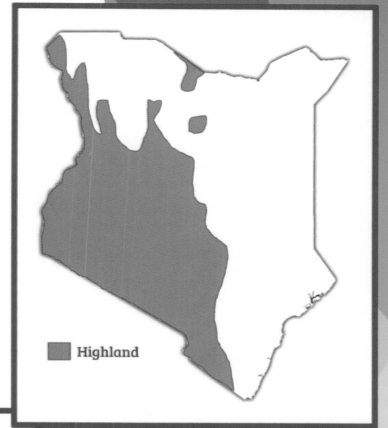

Highland

Areas with the most suitable soil

Some help

- Building and farming in National parks and nature reserves is strictly prohibited and so you will not be able to build in those areas.
- You may find more than one area is suitable and it may be a large area or a small area.
- The rainfall map shows the least places suitable for growing tea so that might be a good place to start.
- Making your decision is only half of the problem, justifying the decision is just as important. Think about why you have selected the areas you have.
- Produce a map to show the location and write a paragraph to justify your chosen area.
- Split the work up between you and your partner so that you can work quickly.

Geography skill covered in this activity:

Using maps in decision making.

30

Farming in Kenya

Farming in Kenya takes place in many ways but one way which has a large impact, both on the people and the environment, is the use of large plantations growing one crop. In Kenya, the land and the climate in the south west of the country are ideal for growing tea. So much so, that Kenya is now the third largest tea producer in the world.

Advantages of large farms

Growing in large farms like these tea plantations leads to lower prices of the tea for the consumer and higher production for the farmer. The larger farms are also very efficient, which means that they can grow a larger amount of tea in a given amount of space than a small farm would. The tea produced in Kenya is largely sold abroad earning Kenya large export revenues. The plantations also employ thousands of people.

Tea plantations in Kenya can be very big.

Disadvantages of large farms

Large tea plantations lead to a loss of biodiversity. This means that there is less variety of plants and animals. They also lead to a loss of habitat to the animals that lived there before the tea plantation was created. There is often a quicker spread of pests and diseases in plantations and the health of the soil decreases over time. The tea plant is not native to Kenya and so the local animals find it hard to adapt.

Do you think large plantations are good or bad?
What are the reasons for your view?

Your tasks:
Using a ruler, copy the table below into your exercise book. Complete the table by adding the statements listed below to the correct column.

Large plantations are good for Kenya	Large plantations are bad for Kenya

Copy these statements into your table.

Draw this in your exercise book. Make your table large enough to fill up your whole page.

Loss of habitats For animals	Few local animals can adapt to the non-native plants being introduced.	Much cheaper to produce large quantities so lower prices
Loss of biodiversity. There is less variety of plants.	Soil health diminishes over time.	Big export earner, earning lots of money from foreign trade.
Tea plantations drain soil of specific nutrients needed by tea plant.	Quicker spread of diseases. One disease can wipe out whole crop.	Provides employment opportunities.
Increase in amount produced.	Tree plants can grow on steep sided hills where other crops cannot.	Higher productivity. Can grow more in a fixed area than small farms.

 There are good points and bad points about using large plantations. Having looked at both sides, what is your overall view? Discuss this with the person next to you.

Geography skill covered in this activity:

 Summarise opposing views

Your tasks:
Write a few sentences to explain whether you think large plantation farms are, overall, a good thing or a bad thing.

Learning objective:

Today we are going to learn what sustainable development is.

Sustainable development.

Sustainable development is a way to use resources without the resources running out. It is a way to meet the needs of the present without harming the ability of future generations to meet their own needs.

? Discuss with your partner. 'Everyone wants a better place to live'. What would you want to make you place a better place to live?

Some people want better homes, while others want better schools. Some people want more jobs, better shops or cleaner and safer streets.

We can group all these desires into three main groups.
- A better environment.
- A better economy.
- Better social conditions.

Sustainable development aims to improve the economy without harming the environment. Or similarly, improving our society without damaging the economy.

These three parts of our world are now seen as being very connected to each other.

Using oil for electricity is good for the economy (cheap) but it is not good for the environment or future generations so using oil is not sustainable.

Using solar power for electricity is more expensive, however, it is good for the environment and for future generations. Solar power is more sustainable than oil.

Can you tell the difference between things that are part of the environment and things that are part of the economy?

Your tasks:

Using a ruler, copy the table below into your exercise book. Complete the table by adding the statements listed below to the correct column.

A better environment	A better economy	A better society

Copy these statements into your table.

Draw this in your exercise book. Make your table large enough to fill up your whole page.

Green spaces	Good leisure facilities	Good, quick, public transport
Friendly neighbours	No litter, no graffiti	Cheaper heat and light
Lots of jobs	Nice gardens, decent houses	Open spaces, Play areas
Less noise and pollution	Reasonable prices	Lots of community groups

In 2008, Oxfam, a charity in the UK, noticed that the Maasai way of life was very sustainable. They build their homes from local materials, eat locally sourced food and they have a stronger culture of reusing and recycling. They are not large users of electicity and they do not travel great distances by ship or plane. It is not suggested that everyone should follow a Maasai way of life. It is suggested that we could learn more from the Maasai about how to live sustainably.

Geography skill covered in this activity:

Classifying statements

Your tasks:

In your own words, describe what sustainable development means to you.

Learning objective:

Understand the
similarities
and differences
between
different
countries.

Similarities and differences.

Kenya is a large country with a warm climate. Home to 54 million people, it sits on the Indian ocean by the equator in East Africa. It has large lakes, mountain ranges, volcanoes and the North East of the country is hot and dry, like a desert.

How does this compare to where you live? Is the country you live in larger or smaller than Kenya? And does your country have a larger or smaller population than Kenya?

Your task:
Look at the facts about Kenya listed below. Using reference books and the internet where available, see how the similar facts for your country compare.

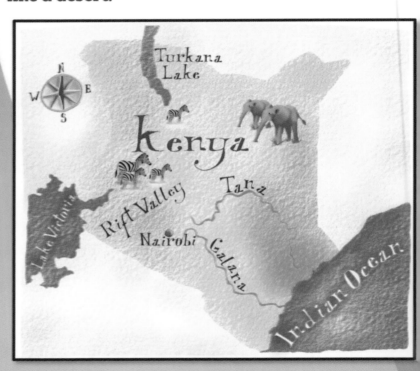

Kenya Fact File

Population:	54, 685, 000 people
Life expectancy	69 years
Official languages:	English and Swahili
Main religion:	Christianity 82%
Land area:	580, 370 square km
Capital city:	Nairobi

Kenyan currency – the Shilling.

Kenyan currency:	Shillings
Highest mountain:	Mount Kenya 5,199 m
Longest river:	Tana river 1,000 km
Largest lake:	Lake Victoria

Lake Victoria.

What have you learnt about Kenya so far?
What things are similar in Kenya to where you live?
What things are different in Kenya to where you live?

Task One:
Copy the table below. Write or draw something that is different and something that is the same about living in Kenya and living where you do.

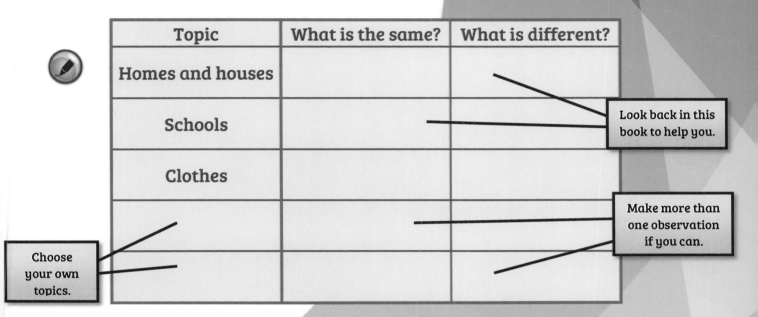

Topic	What is the same?	What is different?
Homes and houses		
Schools		
Clothes		

Look back in this book to help you.

Make more than one observation if you can.

Choose your own topics.

What would you like to find out that you have not learnt yet?
How would you find out something that you want to know?
What are the different ways in which you can find something out?

Task Two:
Make a list of ten facts about Kenya that you have found out for yourself.
You can use reference books, the internet, ask an adult or an older child.
Present your information in a creative way.

Your list of facts could include information on:
- Which countries lie next to Kenya?;
- What the major cities are;
- National customs or traditions in Kenya;
- What the three most popular religions are;
- How long people live for.

What will you find information on?

Geography skill covered in this activity:

Using reference materials to find out information.

Tourism in Kenya

Tourism is a big industry in Kenya. It is the second largest foreign money earner after agriculture and it employs many thousands of people. Kenya is famous for its beautiful white sand beaches and the sense of awe and wonder felt when visiting one of the nineteen national parks in Kenya.

The national parks of Kenya contain many wild animals and stunning scenery which attract people from all over the world.

Kenya is home to many beautiful lakes and the wildlife that inhabit them. Did you know? A flamingo gets more pink, the healthier it is and they can become almost red in colour.

The breath taking scenery of the rift valley is sometimes best witnessed at dawn, when the animals are at their most active. Staying in a tent is a popular way to explore the rift valley although the tents have improved over time to become very comfortable indeed.

The beaches in Kenya are famed for their white sands and beautiful clear blue sea. The beaches are also less busy than more frequently visited beaches in other tourist destinations. For those feeling active, there are plenty of opportunities to enjoy waterskiing, wind surfing, kite surfing and much more. As Kenya is by the equator, the weather is hot all year round and it is popular with tourists from Europe who like to escape the cold winter.

The Kenyan people are famed for their friendly warm service and their happy relaxed atmosphere. Ideal for when people are on holiday.

Discuss with the person next to you, what makes a good holiday destination?

Your tasks:

Either - Design a travel brochure to advertise Kenya as a holiday destination. Add images that capture the beauty and write in persuasive language.

Or - Plan your own itinerary of what you would do if you were to visit Kenya. Think of how long you would go for, what you would do and where would you stay. Where possible, use real travel brochures to help you.

Geography skill covered in this activity:

Reason why some locations favour certain activities.

38

Tourism in Kenya

Learning objective:

Today we are going to learn about tourism in Kenya and why Kenya is a good location for tourism.

One of the big attractions of visiting Kenya is seeing the 'Big Five' animals. The big five are: lion, African elephant, Cape buffalo, Leopard and rhinoceros. The term 'big five' has two meanings.

Originally it refers to the five most difficult animals in Africa to hunt on foot. This was decided by how difficult they were to hunt and the level of danger involved.

It now, however, has a much less sinister meaning and is used by safari tour operators to indicate the animals that they hope will be seen whilst on safari. Countries where all the big five can be seen in the wild include: Botswana, Uganda, Namibia, Ethiopia, South Africa, Kenya, Tanzania, Zimbabwe, DR Congo and

Your tasks:

Make a photo collage like the one above to display the 'Big Five' animals. You could include names and facts to add to your work.

? Can you find out which animals are in danger of becoming extinct? How would you find this out?

Your tasks:

Using the internet to help you, find images of the Kenya that capture its beauty and spirit. Then collate them to make a collage. A collage is where many pictures are joined together to make a new image. Your collage should capture the natural beauty of the Kenyan landscape.

This is a photo collage of Kenyan animals.

You can print off your pictures and cut them out to stick them together with a glue stick. Or, you could use an online software like www.befunky.com which has a collage setting.

Art skill covered in this activity:
To become familiar with the collage technique of art production.

What images could be joined together?
Could you give your artwork an overall theme?
For example, animals? Or sunsets?
Or a particular colour? Or a time of year?

Impressive nature

Africa is big, and it is often under appreciated by many how big it really is. And that size is witnessed in many aspects of life. Here we can see some of the wonders of nature that you can find in Kenya.

The herd of wildebeest in the Maasai Mara National Park is estimated to be at least 1,500,000 in size. Here they are migrating in the search for food.

The flamingos in Kenya can swarm in groups as large as one million and are best seen at Lake Nukuru or Lake Bogoria. Flamingos often stand on one leg and scientists have yet to work out why.

Your tasks:
Search for and collect pictures and facts about the wildebeest or flamingos in Kenya. Decide how you will present your information.

Impressive nature

Vultures have excellent senses of sight and smell to help them locate food, and they can find a dead animal from a mile or more

Cheetahs are the fastest animal in the world. At 114 km per hour, they can outrun a car.

Buffalo are reported to kill more hunters in Africa than any other animal. They are known to ambush hunters that have wounded or injured them.

If it feels threatened, the impala can jump nine metres away to escape danger.

1.80 m at birth, baby giraffes are taller than most adults and can run within hours of

Although hippos might look a little chubby, they can easily outrun a human. Hippos can be extremely aggressive.

Geography skill covered in this activity:

Research for information to justify an opinion.

Your tasks:
'Nature is impressive and deserves our respect'. Using reference books and the internet, find ten interesting facts about Kenyan animals that support this statement. Decide how you will record your findings.

Glossary

Big five

The big five originally refers to the five animals that were most difficult to hunt: lion, elephant, buffalo, leopard and rhinoceros. It is now used by the safari industry to describe the 'must see' animals when on safari.

Climate

Climate means the usual condition of the atmosphere over a long period of time. It refers to the temperature, rainfall, wind strength and humidity. It is different from weather.

Ethnic

An ethnic group is a group of people who are considered to be the same in some way. They may all have the same ancestors, speak the same language, or have the same religion.

Kenya is known for its stunning landscapes.

Environment

The surroundings in which people live. It can refer to the plants, animals and people. It looks at the connections between people and where they live.

Farming

Farming is the raising of food and animals for eating later or to sell for money to buy other necessities. In Kenya, the main crops are coffee and tea.

The great animal migration in Kenya.

Great migration

In Kenya, the great migration refers to the moving of millions of animals in search of food. Every year, wildebeest, zebra, gazelles and other animals move towards more fertile feeding areas after the rains. The animals that feed on them also move.

Landscape

An area of land as one can see it. It includes: the shape of the land, the plants and the animals, the people and their settlements.

Land-use map

A land use map shows the dominant activity in any given area of land.

Maasai

The Maasai are an ethnic group of people that live in Kenya and in the north of Tanzania. They are well known for the way that they dress and their traditional lifestyle.

Nomad

Nomadic people (or nomads) are people who move from one place to another, instead of living in one

A tea plantation in Kenya.

Plantations

A plantation is a large farm which is specialized in farming one type of crop. The crops grown on plantations are usually to sell overseas and not for local use. Kenya has large tea plantations and large coffee plantations.

Rural

A rural area is an area that is not a town or a city, it is often but not always a farming area. It can have small settlements like a hamlet or

Swahili

The Swahili language is a a language spoken throughout East Africa. It is an official language In Kenya and Tanzania.

Tourism

People who travel for fun are called tourists and places that lots of tourists travel to are called resorts. The tourism industry includes travel, places to stay and places to eat. Tourism is a big industry in Kenya.

Urban

Urban means 'Of the town' and it is the opposite to rural. Many people live together in urban areas like towns or cities.

Want to know more? Why not look online!

Index

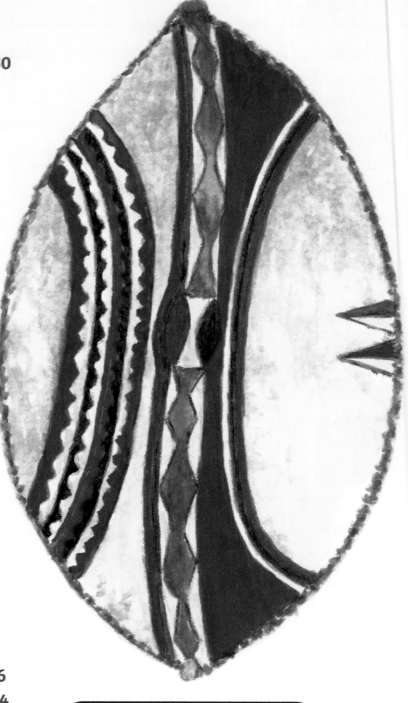

Your tasks:
Research what Maasai shields look like and design one of your own using similar Maasai patters.

Printed in Great Britain
by Amazon

20617967R00029